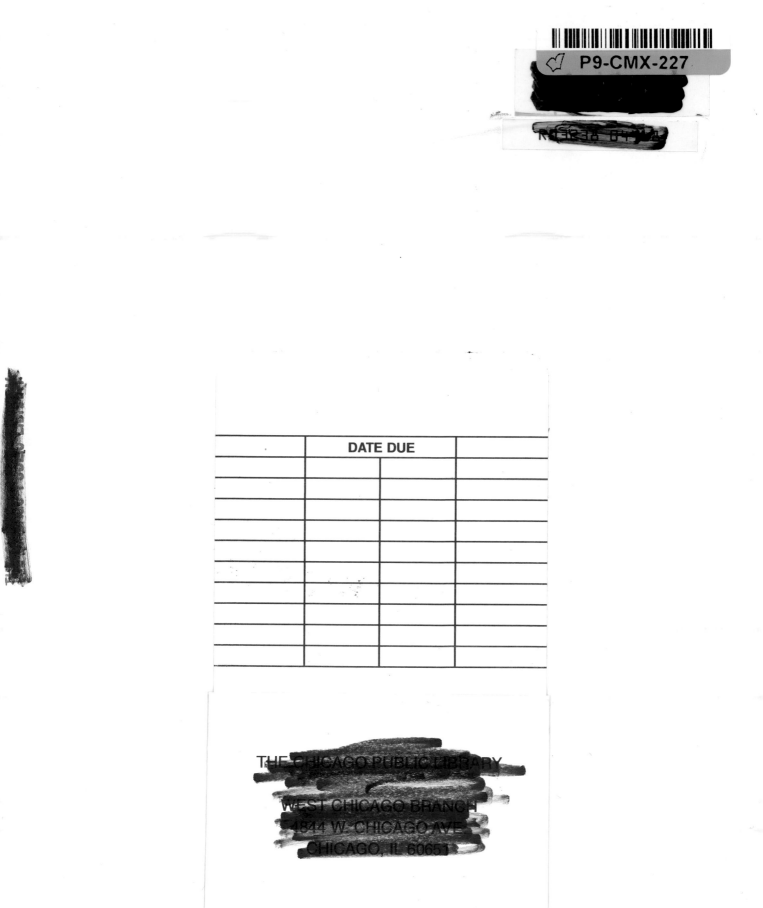

HIGH-SPEED TRAINS
THE NEED FOR SPEED

Chris Maynard

LERNER
SPORTS
AN IMPRINT OF LERNER PUBLISHING GROUP

CREDITS

First American edition published in 2002 by LernerSports

Original edition published 2001 by Franklin Watts

This book is available in two editions:
Library binding by LernerSports
Soft cover by First Avenue Editions
Imprints of Lerner Publishing Group
241 First Avenue North
Minneapolis, MN 55401 U.S.A.
Website address: www.lernerbooks.com

Picture credits: Front cover: top left Milepost 92^1/$_2$ (Brian Solomon), top right Railfotos/Millbrook House Limited (Hugh Ballantyne), middle right Railfotos/Millbrook House Limited (Peter J Howard), bottom Milepost 92^1/$_2$ (Kevin Truby), Back cover: Milepost 92^1/$_2$ (main Brian Solomon; inset Kevin Truby), 1 Milepost 92^1/$_2$ (main AJ Finch), 2-3 Milepost 92^1/$_2$, 4-5 Milepost 92^1/$_2$ (main Brian Solomon), 6-7 Peter Newark's American Pictures, 8-9 Milepost 92^1/$_2$ (main and inset WA Sharman), 10-11 Milepost 92^1/$_2$ (main Kevin Truby; inset Brian Dobbs), 12-13 Milepost 92^1/$_2$ (main and inset Brian Solomon), 14-15 Milepost 92^1/$_2$, 16-17 Milepost 92^1/$_2$ (main Brian Lovell; insets Paul Quayle, AJ Finch), 18-19 Milepost 92^1/$_2$ (main Brian Solomon), 20-21 Milepost 92^1/$_2$, 22-23 Milepost 92^1/$_2$ (main Mark Brayford), 24-25 Eurotunnel, 26-27 Milepost 92^1/$_2$, 28-29 Milepost 92^1/$_2$ (AJ Finch), 30-31 left Peter Newark's American Pictures, middle, right and inset Milepost 92^1/$_2$, 32 Milepost 92^1/$_2$

Library of Congress Cataloging-in-Publication Data

Maynard, Christopher, 1952-
  High-speed trains / by Christopher Maynard.
     p. cm. — (The need for speed)
Includes index.
Summary: Describes the world's high speed passenger trains, from steam engines of the 1930s, through modern supertrains powered by electricity, to magnetic levitation trains now being tested.
  ISBN 0-8225-0387-5 (lib. bdg.)
  ISBN 0-8225-0390-5 (pbk.)
1. High speed ground transportation—Juvenile literature. 2. High speed trains—Juvenile literature. [1. High speed trains.
2. Railroads—Trains.] I. Title. II. Series.
  TF1455 .M39 2002
  625.1—dc21   2001003362

Bound in the United States of America
1 2 3 4 5 6 – OS – 07 06 05 04 03 02

CONTENTS

4 – 5 **INTRODUCTION**

6 – 7 **HIAWATHA**

8 – 9 **MALLARD**

10 – 11 **FLYING SCOTSMAN**

12 – 13 **PIONEER ZEPHYR**

14 – 15 **TRANS EUROPE EXPRESS**

16 – 17 **SHINKANSEN**

18 – 19 **TGV**

20 – 21 **PENDOLINO**

22 – 23 **INTER CITY EXPRESS**

24 – 25 **LE SHUTTLE**

26 – 27 **EUROSTAR**

28 – 29 **MAGLEV**

30 **USEFUL CONTACTS**

31 **TECHNICAL TERMS**

32 **INDEX**

If you and your family ever want to travel faster on land than in a Porsche or a Ferrari, there's a really easy way to do it. Just jump on a train.

Superexpress trains thunder along so fast they make sports cars look like they're going backward. In fact, there isn't a single police car in the world that could catch these trains for speeding. Why? Because on any ordinary day of the week, you can find dozens of trains like these belting along at up to 185 miles per hour (297 kilometers per hour).

High-speed trains have been around in Europe for 20 years and in Japan for twice as long. But that doesn't mean no one tried to set speed records before that. As far back as the 1890s, engineers were trying to nudge their big, clanking steam locomotives up to 100 mph (160 km/h).

But the trouble with steam locomotives is that getting the wheels to go around faster is a tough job. Diesels changed all that, as did electric loco-motives. Modern electric trains take power from overhead cables and are incredibly fast. They whisk passengers nonstop from city to city faster than most airlines. Already they have made test runs with existing trains at much more than 200 mph (321 km/h), and designers are working on models that can break 300 mph (482 km/h).

As well as telling the story of how trains have become the fastest passenger vehicles on land, The Need for Speed also gives you facts and figures about these amazing machines. Look for the boxes marked Stat File and Fact File.

STAT FILE

HIAWATHA

Wheelbase length	78.8 ft (24 m)
Weight (engine)	140 tons (127 tonnes)
Wheel arrangement	4-4-2 (Atlantic)
Fuel	Oil
Cruising speed	100 mph (160 km/h)
Top speed	120 mph (193 km/h)
First run	May 29, 1935

Fact Files give
you slightly unusual,
strange, or funny information.

FACT FILE

Some steam engines carried their fuel (coal or oil) and water in a car called a tender that hitched to the locomotive. Other locomotives, called tank engines, carried their fuel in a storage compartment built around the outside of the locomotive.

When steam trains first began to hit speeds of 100 mph (160 km/h), no one had yet invented a system that was capable of accurately measuring their performance.

The first claim of reaching a speed of more than 100 mph came from the United States in 1893. Then, in 1904, a British company boasted that one of its trains also went this fast. But no one could prove either speed record.

Hitting "100" by luck was one thing. Building a train meant to go that fast was quite another. The very first train that was actually intended to travel at 100 mph was the Hiawatha service. It ran between Chicago and Minneapolis-Saint Paul starting in 1935. Sleek orange, silver, and maroon locomotives hauled the cars on this line. The locomotive's partly covered 7-foot (2-meter) driving wheels and the train's smooth, streamlined finish cut down wind resistance. Even the train's smokestacks were designed to allow air to slip by smoothly.

On a scheduled run, the Hiawatha averaged 80 mph (129 km/h) over the 412-mile (663-kilometer) trip—still a world record for a steam train run between any two stations.

STAT FILE

HIAWATHA	
Wheelbase length	78.8 ft (24 m)
Weight (engine)	140 tons (127 tonnes)
Wheel arrangement	4-4-2
Fuel	Oil
Cruising speed	100 mph (160 km/h)
Top speed	120 mph (193 km/h)
First run	May 29, 1935

It's a Hiawatha Year!

Hiawatha Routes

THE MILWAUKEE ROAD

The distinctive, glass-roofed Skytop Lounge shown in the illustration is a new type of observation room for trackside to mountain top scenic views. Skytop Lounges are carried on the Morning and Afternoon Twin Cities HIAWATHAS and soon will appear on the Olympian HIAWATHA. These cars typify the advanced styling of other Speedlined equipment included in The Milwaukee Road's extensive car building program.

New cars now on the rails have permitted the presentation of improved and new Hiawathas now operating nine thousand miles a day. Additional new cars, scheduled for early delivery, will result in the further amplification of Hiawatha service.

All the new cars embody the latest design and engineering improvements to make your travel hours even more pleasant on "the friendly Railroad of the friendly West". H. Sengstacken, Passenger Traffic Manager, 708 Union Station, Chicago 6, Illinois.

Steam locomotives saw their glory years in the 1930s, when the engines set some amazing speed records.

Locomotive builders of the time wanted to show how fast their engines could go and gave them streamlined shapes. It signaled to the world that they were serious about speed.

The Mallard was built in Britain. It hauled express trains along the London and North-Eastern Railway. The train began service in the summer of 1938, and a few weeks later, in July, it went on the run that made it famous.

During the trip, it towed an extra carriage, called a dynamometer car, fitted with speed-recording gear. As the Mallard came to a gently sloping stretch of track running south between Grantham, England, and Peterborough, England, it picked up speed to reach 114 mph (183 km/h). Gradually it

Tracks had no speed limits in the 1930s. The trains sped along as fast as the driver and fireman could make them go.

accelerated to 125 mph (201 km/h) and at last, for a few seconds, touched 126 mph (202 km/h). Then it ran at over 120 mph (193 km/h) for the next three miles (five km), before overheating forced the driver to slow down. The top speed of 126 mph (202 km/h) was a new world record. To this day, no other steam train has ever beaten it.

The Mallard holds the record, but other trains came close. In Germany, on level track, a train reached 125.5 mph (201 km/h). Some U.S. railroads claimed runs of 127 mph (204 km/h). But these reports were unofficial and never made it into the record books.

STAT FILE

MALLARD

Length	71 ft (21.6 m)
Width	9 ft (2.7 m)
Height	13.08 ft (3.9 m)
Wheel arrangement	4-6-2 (Pacific)
Crew	2
Normal speed	90 mph (145 km/h)
World record speed	126 mph (202 km/h)

FACT FILE

Some steam engines carried their fuel (coal or oil) and water in a car called a tender that hitched to the locomotive. Other locomotives, called tank engines, carried their fuel in a storage compartment built around the outside of the locomotive.

FLYING SCOTSMAN

In the world of steam trains, the all-time superstar for speed and endurance is the British Flying Scotsman—the name of both a locomotive and an express train service.

The London and North-Eastern Railway's locomotive 4472 entered service in February 1923 on the London to Edinburgh run. The journey was so long that it normally took three different locomotives to complete it. The Flying Scotsman performed so well that five years later it made the first-ever nonstop run between the two cities —an amazing feat. It completed the 393-mi (632-km) journey from Kings Cross Station in London to Waverley Station in Edinburgh in a record-breaking 8 hours and 3 minutes—at that time, the longest nonstop run a steam locomotive had ever made.

STAT FILE

FLYING SCOTSMAN 4472

Length	70.5 ft (21.5 m)
Weight	96.8 tons (87.8 tonnes)
Wheel arrangement	4-6-2 (Pacific)
Driving wheels	6.7 ft (2 m)
Crew	2
First run	1923

For the nonstop Scottish service, crews were not allowed to work long hours without a break. They were relieved at the halfway point and went back to a special compartment in the lead carriage to rest, while a fresh crew took over.

In 1862 the first London to Edinburgh journeys took 10 hours or more. The Flying Scotsman managed them in just over 8 hours. Modern service takes just over 4 hours.

FACT FILE

The Flying Scotsman was a luxury express. Special carriages contained a hairdressing compartment, bar, post office, movie theater, and even a special area where wealthy women could rest and be waited on by female attendants. Passengers on the first run were so impressed that they took a collection for the crew. It raised more than a week's wages for a train crew member at the time.

PIONEER ZEPHYR

After a century of dominating rail travel, steam locomotives finally met unbeatable competition in a new kind of train—the diesel electric.

Diesel electrics defeated steam because they were far more powerful and efficient than anything that had gone before. These locomotives use diesel engines to generate the electricity that powers the locomotive's traction motors.

One of the great successes of the diesel electrics was the Pioneer Zephyr. In 1934 it set a world record with a high-speed dash of 1,015 mi (1,633 km) from Denver, Colorado, to Chicago, Illinois. The "Dawn to Dusk" run, as it was known, took 13 hours and 5 minutes, and it cut more than 12 hours from the previous schedule. Along the way, the Zephyr managed an average speed of 78 mph (125 km/h). On certain stretches, it streaked along at 112 mph (180 km/h).

The Zephyr turned the whole idea of passenger trains on its head. Beautifully streamlined in shape, the carriages were smooth and sleek from end to end. The train was built of gleaming stainless steel that weighed a fraction as much as other locomotives.

To the delight of the railroad company that built it, the Zephyr was so fast, light, and efficient that it slashed the running cost per mile for trains on the route. Lovingly preserved in Chicago, the train was photographed during restoration work.

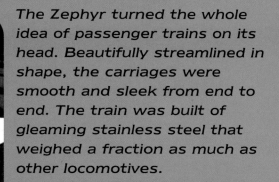

The Zephyr was so sleek and lightweight that it slipped through the air with a third less drag than big, boxy steam engines.

STAT FILE

PIONEER ZEPHYR

Weight	Under 100 tons (90 tonnes)
Engine	Diesel, 660 hp
Traction motors	2 x 300 hp
Crew	2
Top speed	112 mph (180 km/h)

TRANS EUROPE EXPRESS

In 1957 the president of the Netherlands' railways had a wonderful idea. He suggested linking the countries of Europe with a fast, high-class, international railway service.

The Trans Europe Express (TEE) caught on at once. Germany, France, Italy, and Switzerland joined the Netherlands right away. Soon after, Belgium and Luxembourg signed up, too. Spain, Denmark, and Austria came on board a little later. These fast passenger trains offered a regular link between the main cities of Europe. They also aimed to fight off competition from the airlines. Their secret weapons were high speeds and luxurious travel.

TEE trains were supremely comfortable. They had air conditioning, soundproofed cars, double-glazed windows, fine wood paneling, and mirrors. The service had to attract wealthy business travelers, so naturally it was first-class only, with equally first-rate cuisine.

One original idea of the TEE was to let passengers go through customs on the trains. It made border crossings much quicker than the old routine of making passengers disembark and wait to get their passports stamped.

FACT FILE

By the 1980s, high-speed electric trains began to replace the TEEs. The new services had both first-class and second-class cars. They were much bigger and faster than anything that had gone before. The last few diesel TEEs ran until the 1990s, when they were retired from service.

STAT FILE

TRANS EUROPE EXPRESS

Length	315 ft (96 m)
Weight	278 tons (253 tonnes)
Power	2,000 horsepower twin diesels powering a generator that drove four electric motors
Top speed	87 mph (140 km/h)

Diesel electrics are fast. Faster still are the latest all-electric passenger trains. They reach top speeds that remind us of airplanes rather than of things that run on rails. The grandfather of all modern high-speed trains is Japan's "bullet train" or Shinkansen.

Shinkansen means "new long-distance track" in English. Before the Shinkansen, trains of all types had always shared the same lines. So this was the first dedicated high-speed railroad ever built in the world. It was designed to take passenger trains only.

The first Shinkansen services ran on high-speed lines that stretched from Tokyo to Osaka. They traveled at the monumental cruising speed of 137 mph (220 km/h). The current trains also run to many other parts of Japan. The latest express model, the shark-nosed Nozomi 500 service (shown below) can blast along at more than 187 mph (300 km/h). It's the fastest scheduled train service in the world.

The aerodynamic slope of the latest Shinkansen locomotives easily cuts through wind resistance.

SHINKANSEN

Length	984 ft (300 m)
Width	11 ft (3.3 m)
Power	64 electric motors, one driving each axle and delivering 15,800 horsepower in all
Top speed	137 mph (220 km/h)

Since 1993 Shinkansen test trains running on existing lines have been regularly reaching speeds of well over 250 mph (402 km/h).

The rounded nose of the first models earned them the nickname "bullet train." The design was inspired by the shape of the front of a DC-8 airliner, which represented state-of-the-art air travel 35 years ago.

TRAIN A GRANDE VITESSE

On September 27, 1981, a bright orange supertrain slipped out of the station for its first public journey from Paris to Lyon in France. The new train was known as the TGV, and the age of high-speed train travel in Europe had begun.

TGV stands for "Train à Grande Vitesse" or "High-Speed Train." The name also refers to the special lines and the ultramodern signaling that let it run at the terrific speed of 186 mph (300 km/h). TGV is a whole high-speed system.

The first service from Paris to Lyon was such a success that it wiped out the airline business on this busy route. TGVs link Paris to Brussels, Belgium; to Amsterdam, the Netherlands; and to London, England, in the north and to Marseilles and Bordeaux in the south of France. Other countries, like Spain and South Korea, have also begun to buy the supertrain that reinvented passenger travel.

FACT FILE

On May 18, 1990, a "souped-up" TGV set a new world speed record. In tests to find out how fast steel wheels on steel rails could go, it thundered up and down a section of brand-new track. The train performed amazingly and clocked 322 mph (518 km/h). However, there's no chance of us traveling this fast in the near future. Modern brakes simply can't manage at these speeds.

STAT FILE

TGV

Length	656 ft (200 m)
Width	9.5 ft (2.9 m)
Height	13 ft (4.0 m)
Weight	424 tons (385 tonnes)
Engines	12 electric motors delivering 8,650 horsepower
Top speed	186 mph (300 km/h)

PENDOLINO

Why do motorcyclists lean into curves? It's to stop themselves from flying off as they go around a bend.

Pendolino trains lean into curves, too. This Italian train has a clever system of controls that tilts the passenger carriages whenever they go around a bend at high speed and stops the passengers from flying around inside. The tilt can be as much as eight degrees from upright, but for the travelers within, everything feels normal and comfortable.

Because of this, a Pendolino train can zip along an existing railway line more than a third faster than other trains. It can round curves at full speed and cut many minutes off long-distance journeys.

The first carriage of the train has a "brain" that senses when a curve is coming up. A computer measures what is happening, and in a split second it leans each carriage toward the inside of the curve. The system works so well that it can even handle S-curves. The front carriages tilt right while the back ones are still leaning to the left!

FACT FILE

When a train rounds a bend quickly, centrifugal force flings passengers outward from the curve. This is the same kind of force that slams you hard against the sides of a banking roller coaster. Tilting the train on curves cuts the force so much that passengers (and food and drink) hardly wobble at all.

STAT FILE

PENDOLINO ETR 450

Length	793 ft (242 m)
Seating	344 passengers
Weight	474 tons (430 tonnes)
Power	6,680 horsepower from 12 electric motors
Top speed	155 mph (250 km/h)

INTER CITY EXPRESS

In Germany the new generation of supertrains is known as *Inter City Express (ICE)*. They first went into service in 1991. They run on upgraded existing railroad lines or on special high-speed tracks.

The trains are three times as long as a soccer field and seat 645 passengers. Most of them have 12 carriages and two locomotives, one in front and one at the rear. At the end of the line, the crew simply switches ends, so there's no need to uncouple and move locomotives around.

The first new trains could hustle along at 175 mph (280 km/h). Newer ones go even faster. The latest ICEs have a top speed of 206 mph (330 km/h).

To go this fast, the trains must be as streamlined as airplanes. That's why the locomotives have sloping fronts with rounded noses and why each car is linked to the next by an airtight seal. No windows can be opened either, otherwise at high speeds, the blast would bounce passengers around like ping-pong balls.

STAT FILE

INTER CITY EXPRESS

Length	1,174 ft (358 m)
Width	10 ft (3 m)
Height	14 ft (4.3 m)
Weight	880 tons (798 tonnes)
Top speed	174 mph (280 km/h)

Modern electrics pick up power from overhead cables with a steel arm, called a pantograph, on the roof. Because they don't need to haul a heavy diesel engine, the locomotives are much lighter. These factors help make the trains very fast.

Before it went into service, the ICE had to undergo thorough testing. During one run on a high-speed line in 1988, it reached 254 mph (409 km/h). For a short while, this stood as a world record.

Deutsche Bahn AG
Forschungs- und Technologiezentrum

410 101-0

LE SHUTTLE

Underground trains run mostly beneath city streets. They may beat the traffic jams above, but they are pretty slow as they trundle between stations. However, the fastest underground train in the world, by far, is Le Shuttle.

Le Shuttle, the name of a fleet of supertrains, runs back and forth between England and France through the Channel Tunnel. Le Shuttle only has two stops, one at each end of the 30-mile (48-km) tunnel. It glides through in 35 minutes, reaching speeds of 87 mph (140 km/h) along the way. On a normal day, one of these big trains will make about 20 crossings.

Le Shuttle trains haul cars, buses, trucks, trailers, and motorcycles, since there is no way for these vehicles to drive directly through the tunnel. The system can handle a train leaving the terminal every 15 minutes at peak times. During these rushes, two shuttles run through the tunnel in each direction at the same time.

STAT FILE

LE SHUTTLE TRAIN

Length	About 2,400 ft (731 m)
Width	8.8 ft (2.7 m)
Weight	2,645 tons (2,400 tonnes)
Full load	120 cars & 12 buses (about 1,000 passengers)
Locomotives	2 electric locomotives, one at each end
Power (each loco)	7,600 hp
Top speed	87 mph (140 km/h)

FACT FILE

A tunnel that lies under the seabed sounds dangerous. What if it leaks? As it happens, all underwater tunnels leak. But they are built in such a way that the water is collected and pumped out. The Channel Tunnel has a system of powerful pumps that can cope with any water that dribbles into it.

Boarding Eurostar is more like getting on an airplane than in a train.

The check-in looks like an airport. The staff wear Eurostar uniforms and speak several languages. Announcements to passengers are in English, French, and on some routes, Flemish (the language spoken in northern Belgium). Even the drivers have to speak several languages so they can talk to the controllers along the way.

The train itself looks as sleek as a space shuttle. Under the skin, it's also a miracle of modern engineering. It is built from the same basic plan as the TGV. And, like the TGV, it runs incredibly fast, though only in France and Belgium where there is a high-speed line. In Britain, it travels more slowly because of the old-fashioned power system and tight curves on the line.

Even so, Eurostar has linked London, England, to Paris, France, and Brussels, Belgium, in about three hours. That's fast enough to compete easily with scheduled airlines.

STAT FILE

EUROSTAR

Length	1,292 ft (394 m)
Width	9 ft (2.8 m)
Weight	828 tons (752 tonnes)
Engines	12 electric motors delivering 16,300 horsepower
Top speed	186 mph (300 km/h)

The nose of the train is sloped to slip through the Channel Tunnel with the least discomfort to passengers. The train is sealed against the sharp changes of pressure outside it.

FACT FILE

The Eurostar is the most complex train in the world because it has to work in three countries and the Channel Tunnel, all of which have different operating conditions. So the train takes to the rails with three power supplies, four signaling systems, and staff members who speak at least three different languages.

MAGLEV

A train that floats above the ground and scoots along without wheels sounds like science fiction, but it exists.

The Japanese have been testing Maglev trains that are lifted, guided, and propelled by supermagnets since the early 1970s. More than 30 years later, things are still at the testing stage, but they have come a long way.

The biggest success so far has been the MLX01. This three-carriage train runs on the Yamanashi Maglev Test Line (shown in the main picture). The lead carriages at either end of the train are streamlined. The train can be driven manned or unmanned.

Maglev stands for "magnetic levitation." The MLX01 is packed with powerful superconducting magnets. As they pass the magnetic coils that line the sides and bottom of the track, three things happen. The train is lifted off the ground. It is gripped smack in the center of the track (so it doesn't bump into the walls), and it powers forward at incredible speed.

Early Maglev vehicles looked boxy and unstreamlined.

STAT FILE

MAGLEV

Length	255 ft (78 m)
Weight	87 tons (79 tonnes)
Top speed	345 mph (555 km/h)

FACT FILE

Maglev trains have some big downfalls. First, the track costs a lot of money to build. Second, the system uses a huge amount of electricity. Third, it creates very powerful magnetic fields. You couldn't run a laptop computer onboard, because the magnetic field would scramble the computer's chips.

USEFUL CONTACTS

If you want to find out more about any of the trains in this book, here are a few useful places to start looking.

Association of Railway Museums
P.O. Box 370
Tujunga, California 91043
email: secretary@railwaymuseums.org
website: www.railwaymuseums.org

Flying Scotsman Railways
Castle Farm, Lavendon
Buckinghamshire MK46 4JG
England
email: info@flyingscotsman.com
website: www.flyingscotsman.com

Museum of Science and Industry
Pioneer Zephyr Exhibit
5700 South Lake Shore Drive
Chicago, Illinois 60637
website: www.msichicago.org/
exhibit/zephyr

WEBSITES

American Society of Mechanical Engineers
www.asme.org/history/topics.html#Rail

Eurostar
www.eurostar.com

Japan Railways Group
www.japanrail.com

National Railway Museum
www.nrm.org.uk

Steam Locomotive Dot Com
www.steamlocomotive.com

The Stockton and Darlington Railway
www.railcentre.co.uk

Train à Grande Vitesse
www.tgv.com

The Website for the Railway Industry
www.railway-technology.com

WORLD SPEED RECORDS: TRAINS

Fastest steam locomotive A4 Class Mallard, Britain	July 3, 1938	126 mph (202 km/h)
Fastest diesel train InterCity 125, Britain	Nov 1, 1987	148 mph (237 km/h)
Fastest electric train TGV-A Set 325, France	May 18, 1990	322 mph (515 km/h)
Fastest Maglev train MLX01 Maglev, Japan	April 14, 1999	345 mph (552 km/h)
Fastest scheduled speed between two stations 500 Series, Japan	March 1997	164 mph (262 km/h)
Fastest rail vehicle (any kind) Unmanned rocket sled, United States	1982	6,157 mph (9,851 km/h)

TECHNICAL TERMS

axle-loading: the weight on the track of a locomotive's heaviest set of wheels

bogie: a truck with a set of wheels, usually four, that pivots under the frame of a locomotive or coach

class: a category of locomotives that have all been built to the same design

compound locomotive: a steam locomotive in which the steam flows through a high-pressure and then a low-pressure cylinder in order to get every ounce of power from the engine

cylinders: the two or more chambers of a steam locomotive where moving pistons, pushed by steam, pump back and forth to rotate the driving wheels

diesel electric: a class of locomotive that uses both diesel engines and electric motors to provide power

first class: Since the earliest days passenger compartments have been divided into different classes. First is always the most comfortable and most expensive. Second class is sometimes referred to as standard class. In past times, there were third and even fourth classes with hard wooden benches and very cheap prices.

gauge: the width of a railroad track, measured between the insides of the two rails

generator: the unit that generates electricity in a diesel-electric locomotive. It is powered by a diesel engine.

locomotive: the vehicle of a train that moves the railroad cars with its own supply of power.

pantograph: the metal antennae on electric trains that stick up from the roof. They collect electricity from overhead cables and feed it to the motors.

power supply: the voltage supplied to electric trains. It varies from one country to another. It can be as low as 750 volts delivered by a third rail in Britain and up to 25,000 volts supplied by overhead cables in France.

tender: a small wagon coupled behind a steam locomotive that carries the fuel—usually coal or oil—and water to make steam.

traction motor: a motor that usually sits low, next to the wheels, and gets its "juice" from either a generator or from overhead electric cables

wheel arrangement: the set-up of leading wheels, driving wheels, and trailing wheels written down as a three number formula, for example, 2-4-0. The figures show how many of each kind of wheel a steam locomotive has.

Belgium, 14, 26
brakes, 18
Britain, 6, 8, 10, 26
Brussels, Belgium, 18, 26
bullet train. *See* Shinkansen

carriages, 8, 11, 12, 14, 16, 22, 28
Channel Tunnel, 24-25, 26, 27
crews, 8, 11, 26

diesel-electric locomotives, 4, 12-13, 14-15
dynamometer car, 8

Edinburgh, Scotland, 10, 11
electricity, 14, 29
electric locomotives, 4, 16-21, 22
Europe, 4, 22
Eurostar, 26-27

Flying Scotsman, 10-11
France, 14, 18, 19, 24, 26

Germany, 14, 22

Hiawatha, 6-7

Inter City Express (ICE), 22-23
Italy, 14, 20

Japan, 4, 16-17, 28-29

Le Shuttle, 24-25
locomotive 4472. *See* Flying Scotsman
London, England, 10, 11, 18, 26
London and North-Eastern Railway, 8, 10

Maglev, 28-29
magnets, 28
Mallard, 8-9

pantograph, 23
Paris, France, 18, 19, 26
passengers, 11, 14, 16, 18, 20, 22, 24, 26
Pendolino, 20-21
Pioneer Zephyr, 12-13
power supplies, 26, 27

rails, 16, 18. *See also* tracks, railroad

Scotland, 10, 11
Shinkansen, 16-17
signaling, 18, 27
South Korea, 18
Spain, 14, 18
speed records, 4, 6, 8, 12, 17, 18, 20
steam locomotives, 4, 6-11, 12
streamlining, 6, 8, 12, 28

tender, 9, 11
TGV, 18-19, 26
tracks, railroad, 16, 18, 28, 29. *See also* rails
Trans Europe Express (TEE), 14-15

underground trains, 24-25, 26-27

wheels, 6, 7, 28